On the Job

Teachers
In Our Community

Michelle Ames

PowerKiDS press.

New York

Published in 2010 by The Rosen Publishing Group, Inc.
29 East 21st Street, New York, NY 10010

First Edition

Editor: Nicole Pristash
Book Design: Greg Tucker
Photo Researcher: Jessica Gerweck

Photo Credits: Cover, pp. 15, 24 (left) Jose Luis Pelaez/Getty Images; pp. 5, 24 (right-center) © www.istockphoto.com/Nancy Louie; p. 7 Catherine Ledner/Getty Images; pp. 9, 11, 17, 19, 23, 24 (left-center), 24 (right) Shutterstock.com; p. 13 John-Francis Bourke/Getty Images; p. 21 © www.istockphoto.com/Bonnie Jacobs.

Library of Congress Cataloging-in-Publication Data

Ames, Michelle.
  Teachers in our community / Michelle Ames. — 1st ed.
     p. cm. — (On the job)
  Includes bibliographical references and index.
  ISBN 978-1-4042-8069-4 (library binding) — ISBN 978-1-4358-2456-0 (pbk.) — ISBN 978-1-4358-2461-4 (6-pack)
  1. Teachers—Juvenile literature. I. Title.
  LB1775.A44 2010
  371.1—dc22
                                        2008051467

Manufactured in the United States of America

Contents

A teacher's job is to help **students** learn new things.

Teachers work at schools and inside classrooms.

Teachers help their students learn how to read.

When a student needs help with a computer, a teacher shows him what to do.

This teacher is reading to her class. Teachers read from books and **textbooks**.

Teachers even help students learn to play **instruments**!

Art teachers show students how to draw.

Sometimes, a teacher brings her class to a **museum** where there is a lot to learn.

Teachers take time to explain things that are hard to understand.

Teachers help students learn new things every day!

Words to Know

instruments

museum

students

textbooks

Index

Web Sites

Due to the changing nature of Internet links, PowerKids Press has developed an online list of Web sites related to the subject of this book. This site is updated regularly. Please use this link to access the list:
www.powerkidslinks.com/job/teacher/